The Enormity of
Existence

Nolo Segundo

Copyright© 2020 Nolo Segundo
ISBN: 978-93-90202-98-0

First Edition: 2020
Rs. 200/-

Cyberwit.net
HIG 45 Kaushambi Kunj, Kalindipuram
Allahabad - 211011 (U.P.) India
http://www.cyberwit.net
Tel: +(91) 9415091004 +(91) (532) 2552257
E-mail: info@cyberwit.net

Printed at Repro India Limited.

PREFACE

My poems are written rather simply, and clearly. In this I know I go against the grain of much modern poetry that like, its counterpart, abstract art, tends to the recondite and is often so idiosyncratic that the reader may left wondering, what does it mean? I know the zeitgeist is 'to show, don't tell', but I'm not sure how much modern poetry is showing anyone. Some of the greatest poets, Homer, Shakespeare, the Psalmists, told us about ourselves as sentient beings with our unique awareness of the Universe and our endless attempts to understand our place in it. Hamlet's angst as expressed in 'to be or not to be' could only apply to human beings as animals do not commit suicide. Since the time he wrote those lines there has been a secular trend to see homo sapiens as just another species, just another animal. But we are much more—and much less— than animals. For one thing, we lack their innocence – if the shark eats you or the tiger mauls you, that is not evil, but merely instinct. But we have gone far past our instincts, even the one for self-preservation, or why would we have built a world-wide weapons system that can destroy all life in less than an hour? What species in their right mind would ever do such a thing?

Some of these poems are about aging, memory, and of course love— what true poet doesn't write about love? But many go against the secular trend of materialism— the idea, belief really, that only matter is real: no God, no soul, and therefore, because we are just 'flukes' in this vast, indifferent Universe, sentient beings born only to become extinct, there is no meaning to life. That must be the take on it if the atheist is honest. I know many people who live that way, and manage to cope, some quite well it seems, living with the absurdity that we appear to be simply born to die—and unlike other animals, we know it.

I saw life that way myself and might still do if I had not suffered a deep clinical depression in the early '70's, the kind where you stop eating, sleeping, taking an interest in anything. Do that and soon enough your nervous system breaks down, and you skake like you have advanced Parkinson's disease.

I believed then that death meant extinction, so to that part of my mind still functioning, it seemed logical to kill myself. So in time I threw myself off a bridge into a spring-swollen river in Vermont [I allude to this in the 'The Leap'.] And then I knew! I knew this world was only one world our souls, that endless consciousness that is in every person you see, inhabit. I also knew that the problem with life is not that it is meaningless, as atheism logically posits, but that there is so much meaning that we can at best only 'access' some of it, through love, through faith, through the good karma we make, and more rarely perhaps though an occasional revelation.

In this I am not talking religion—I worship as a Christian (not a very good one, I'm sure) but I suspect re-incarnation is a reality, as I allude to an incident I experienced as an agnostic 18 year old but discounted at the time, in the poem, 'Gettysburg Redux'. Actually, I am more concerend with what I call faith, or a constant seeking of 'the More', that which is so far beyond us and yet, paradoxically, so much within us that many of us fail to 'see' it, that is God or whatever name you call God. It took the most hellish day of my life for me to start—to just start— to awaken.

So my poems attempt to prompt a little thinking, a little more openess, perhaps even a satori-like awareness; and I am not being disingenuous to disclaim credit if that happens. The truth, the reality is that I have not so much written them as they have written themselves—by way of my soul, I suspect.

Finally, I chose the pen name 'Nolo Segundo' because I like the way it rolls off the tongue, like a tiny poem; I wasn't aware when I picked it that in Latin in means 'I don't want to be second' until my Epsicopal priest pointed it out to me. Well, I suppose that is true for all of us, really—L.J. Carber

CONTENTS

I SING TO ETERNITY

To an unmet friend:

You see the mortal world
And for you man is machine
Little more than a device
For the vagaries of evolution,
Faith is illusion, hope lacks
Weight— and love? Can love
Be other than mere sex,
Nature's sole mandate?

And your science now tells
You: what can I ever know?
All is a quantum topsy-turvy,
And mother nature part
Whore, part illusionist....
Your thinking breaks all
Down to little pieces,
And nothing matters
As matter is all while
Science the only god
Left for us to worship.
And we are nothing,
Not even dreams
Anymore, just bits
And pieces to be
Examined, classified
And then ignored—
For science is all,
And faith but a
Refuge for fools.

You are honest,
I know—you see
Yourself as just
Another machine,
Destined for decay,
Then destruction—
Your sentience but
A cruel joke told
Yet again—and
No one laughs.

You and I,
We breathe,
We think,
We live—but
You would stop
At death while
I begin there....

I sing to the eternal,
Quell not my songs,
As they rise above
The despair born
Of your vacant
World, following
Stars streaming
Their wondrous
Light in a dead-
Cold universe.

I sing to eternity,
I sing to my soul.

EMERGENCE

Once...
I took long walks through the Universe
making giant strides across formless space
(just the way a giant would)
thrilled to think if it never ended
it would yet be too soon.
People took me for a child,
were decieved by simple diguise
for I was seer, prophet, and beggar.

One day
as I was meandering across the Milky Way
movement stopped— I had touched the Fear
and froze fast to It
with all the desperate and mad ardor
of a melting icicle for the roof ledge.

Unseeing days string into beads of blind years—
I became the criminal courting his cell,
a burnt out Prometheus on his boring hill,
an ox of ignorance forever pulling a water wheel
(but there is no water), or to say it another way,
a sleepwalker who dreamt he was awake....

I stopped looking for escape,
turned a key to lock chains that never were
and existed for treading,
the endless treading through nothing

until a push and a long, long falling
through a tunnel filled with nightmare
and madness and tears—suddenly
to awaken like Alice did
from the dreams of ants
to the dreams of Emperors, Kings and Queens.

Now I wear life as a jewel around my neck
and enter only houses with many doors.

c. 2019

FLICKERING THROUGH THE MIND

What flickers through the mind?

A half-thought, never completed?
A line of poetry never written?
A memory of a love long lost?

All the brain's sparkling confetti,
falling into myriad streams
merging into a relentless river
emptying into that black ocean—
the unconscious....

DREAMS AND ETERNITY

My wife had a dream—
We were on a train, and
As it pulled into the station,
She grabbed the bags, but
I had vanished. She looked
And looked, went up and
Down the platform anxiously
As waves of strangers moved
Past her, her fears rising, throat
Drying as she felt abandoned,
Like a child alone in the world.

She went to where the proud
Station master stood, and then
Saw me behind him, looking very
Tired, worn-out, perhaps even sad.

I did not ask her what she thought
The dream might mean, if anything.
But I wondered—if it meant my life
Was closing out, our long train ride
Together was coming to the terminal.
My wife would have to travel alone...
until till she took her own last train.

Was it 'just a dream' or a dream rare,
A dream of prophecy, a dream calling,
A dream of eternity...but isn't every
Dream eternal? Existing like a little

Life, real and of time and substance—
a tease of sorts from the other side.

c. 2018

A PASSING GLANCE

The other day
as I turned the corner
onto my quiet street

I saw a woman so perfect,
she snatched my breath away
as she waited to cross the road.

It was like seeing a movie star
or a beauty queen close up—
my heart ached a bit, I confess,
when I thought, once, a long time
ago, I might have had a chance....

But now I'm just an old man
driving an old car to an old house.
I drove slowly and could see
her gracefully crossing the street
in my rear-view mirror, much
like a dream fading quickly away ...
suddenly, from somwhere far
beyond my mind, I realized
the truth of what I saw: that
it was all just stupid illusion—
she was young and beautiful,
I, old and lame, but those were
just markers on the wheel of time.

The wheel would turn,
my body would die, hers would age,
no longer enrapturing men—in truth
she was already an old woman which
I could not see, nor could I see the
sweet child still playing within her.

When there are no more days left,
our souls will be free of the wheel,
and all the world's illusions will
seem as distant, fading dreams.

c. 2020

ON FINDING A DEAD DEER IN MY BACKYARD

I saw them a few weeks ago.
My wife called me, something urgent—
so I left the computer and went to see
what so excited her.

Three deer, 3 young deer meandering
around our ¼ acre backyard.
They look thin, she said— I agreed
(not saying it was not a good sign
with winter coming near).

We enjoyed watching them
through our plate glass door, their
casual grace, that elegance of walk
deer have when unafraid.
They were special, even more than
the occasional cardinal
alighting in our yard like
a breathing ruby with wings— so
we stayed as still as possible.
I told her that deer can only see
what moves, so we held ourselves
tight, like insensate statues.

Two of these whitetailed beauties
grazed daintyly on the ground
but the third went to our giant hollytree,

resplendent with its myriad red berries,
like necklesses thrown capricious.
I was concerned— something alarming
about even a deer drawn like the proverbial moth—
safe, I wondered, for deer or tree?

The triplets soon left our yard,
as casually as they had come,
and a week went quietly by—
then one day a single deer came back.
I say back because she went straight
for the hollytree, and I banged on the
plate glass door and yelled as fierce as an
old man can yell to scare off the now
unwanted intruder, for something told me
the holly tree would be death to the deer.

She fled, but the next day came back again,
again alone, and again with eyes only
for that tree, an Eve that could not say
no to the forbidden fruit...
or berries or leaves it appears.
Again I chased her away, and
for a few days saw no return.

Then one brisk morning our neighbor called—
he saw what we could not see in the deep green
thickness of that holly tree—the doe lay sleeping
under its canopy (so death always seems with animals
unlike a human corpse where something is gone),
killed it seemed by berries or the leaves of the innocent tree.

I called my township— they said, put the carcass by the street,

we'll send someone to pick it up— but I couldn't , or wouldn't.
Not just because I walk with a cane, and am old and unsure
how such a moving would be done— no, no, it was more—
when I saw the deer lying sheltered beneath the tree it loved,
the tree it died for, it seemed a sacred place, consecrated—
and I could not bring myself to violate nature's holy ground.

Fortunately I have a neighbor who is not sentimental, and he
dragged the dead doe roughly to the curb, and I knew, by
its pungent unearthly smell of death, it was the only answer.

c. 2019

ODE TO MRS. MILLER

I did not know how brave she was—
Ninety-two and I, seventy less,
So young that old age
Was textbook stuff:
A fact of life,
But not mine.

I was alive and free
To stride the world,
A colossus of youth—
Whereas she had ate
Almost a century.
And all her friends
And all her family
Lay dead somewhere—
Except in her mind,
Still crisp, poignant
In its memories
Of a wealthy husband,
A daughter dead young.
Her own youth and beauty
Remain lonely in a
Silver-framed photo.

She never complained,
This old lady—
Never once did I hear
Lamentations, a bewailing
For the richness of life:

The ripe fullness she once felt
As a wife, a mother, a woman
Of grace and beauty.

She lived alone
In a basement flat,
Barely five feet tall—
Yet I've never known
Any being braver—
Yet it is only now,
That I am become old,
I envy such courage.

c. 2016

A CHILD'S CHRISTMAS CAROL

Then... it was a time of true magic,
When the world was small and soft.
It had to be magic, my mind of five
Told me: how else could my brothers
And I go to sleep on an ordinary,
Dull and quiet night, to awaken in
Sheer joy the next morn as though
We had been zapped by a warm
Bolt of harmless lightning, setting
Our now restless bodies tingling....

Like racehorses at the gate of magic,
We stood at the top of the stairs,
Pulling at whatever patience we
Could muster under the admonitions
Of Mom and Dad to wait! wait! the
Camera must be loaded—but how
Painful to be still when we knew
Children's paradise was only a
Stairway away—and what a
Paradise we saw unfolded in
Our now unfamiliar living room!

The tree drew our eyes first—
It was big and fat, with its
Branches sagging under all
Its myriad ornaments: glass
Balls, plastic candy canes,
Tinsel drooping as though
It hung on a weeping willow
And not a proud Blue Spruce.

And hundreds and millions of
Colored lights, some blinking,
Some staid, made our tree
Sparkle like the royal crown
Of a giant king—perhaps
The King of Toys, for they
Were seen in abundance
Wherever we looked: trucks
And bikes, and bats and games.
Each brother had his own pile
(we marveled how thoughtful
Santa must be) and we knew
In each stack there were boxes
Beautifully wrapped but sans

Treasure , hiding only socks
Or shirts, perhaps a sweater.

Well, even the jolly fat man
Could not be perfect—still,
He would bring magic to our
Home every year, overnight
Transforming prosaic lives
By wonder, by magic, by love,
And after he went away,
When I was an ancient six,
The world grew much bigger
But colder, dull and empty
Of that special joy that
Can only come to those
Children who believe....

c. 2015

A SENSE OF GOD

It comes with the light,
Driving darkness to dust,
Breathing life into death,
Freeing all touched softly.

There is a way of seeing
Without eyes, hearing
Beyond human ears,
Smelling a rose before
Its seed is in the earth,
And touching a beating
Heart with unseen hands.

It takes no more than one
Drop of His blood to save
A world lost in madness.

c. 2016

A LETTER FROM GOD

Why are we so stupid, Lord?
Why do we yell and shout,
Rant and rave, pillage and kill?
Why do we cheat and lie,
Ignore and disdain,
Leave and abandon?

We could all be so close,
So loving, so kind.
After all—
We all share the same things:
The fresh air, the blue sky,
The moonlit nights.
We all have the same fears:
Loneliness and sickness,
Poverty and death.

We all hold fast
To the same hopes and dreams—
Friends and family of love, perhaps
Happy children whirling
Like small dervishes
In their own little worlds.
A bit of praise, a kind word,
Work that goes well.

I wrote this as a poem
But it is really a prayer.
I spoke it aloud so many times,

Even unto the thick part
Of the blackest night
Until I fell into a deep sleep.

When I awoke the next morn,
The mail had come early.
I opened an envelope
That had no stamp.
Handwritten in unreal beauty,
It began quite formally:
Dear Mr. and my name,
I have broken my own rule
To write you, but you are
So very persistent!

If life were easy,
You would not feel alive.
If love were easy,
You would not value it.

And if I were easy,
You would never seek me.

Faithfully yours,
God

c. 2016

A SECOND LETTER FROM GOD

I suppose I should have been satisfied
With the first letter—I mean, how
Often does the Almighty write to us?
Not since He did it on stone, I suppose.
But I am human and so rarely content—
Then too, I still had so many questions,
Like why must children suffer cruelty
Or deathly ills—and why are the aged
So oft forgotten, ignored, neglected?
Why do so many hunger for vengeance
While others thirst for a drop of love?

Before the act is always the thought—
So why do we lessen the other, turn
Him into an animal, some predator
To be feared and hunted to extinction?
And why do we peacock ourselves
With plumes of ego and pride, then
Go strutting into the world like
Petty kings, wood-hearted queens?
And always, always, we are we less
Than we could be, sad thin shadows
Of that person we know could, and
Should walk free on the sun-lit earth?

I wrote this unmailed letter knowing
He would read the words before I
Could put them down—but I did
Not expect an answer— so when I
Found another letter slipped under

My door, this too written in a hand
Of unearthly beauty, I gasped with
Guilt and fear—was I too greedy,
Too foolish to want to know the
Mind of God: why He made us
The way we are, what He wants
From us, of us , for us? Now I
Began trembling, my heart
Pounding like it would burst.

Still,
  I opened the letter and read—
'I really am breaking all my own
Rules in writing you again, and
I'm not sure why—yes,
I don't always know my
Own mind—I told you

You were made in my
Image. I suppose I am
Intrigued –the answers
You seek have been
Sought throughout
Time, ever really
Since I put that
Immortal part of you
In your ancestors,
And turned animal
Into human and
Instinct into choice.

I gave your species
Everything needed:
Reason, imagination,

Speech, and my
Greatest gift—love
Strong enough to
Transcend time.
And what did you
Humans do with
All these wonders?
You waged war
Endlessly and
Oppressed the
Weak, breaking
Them as though
They were clay
pots and not
My children....

I sent prophets
To warn you
To chose light
Before the dark
Ate your souls—
I even sent my
Only son to
Lead you home—
But you killed him.
And you wonder
Why life is hard?'

As always,
faithfully yours—
God

c. 2016

IN MY GRANDMOTHER'S DAY

Nana told me once
How she and Pop-pop
Went courting in a
Horse and buggy.

How quaint I thought,
And was a just a bit
Amazed how far we
Humans have gone—
From a smelly plodding
Horse to crossing a vast
Ocean in an afternoon
While six miles high.

Then Grandma told me
Something shocking:
She said they went out
In that carriage to make
Love! Nana! I gasped to
Myself, until I saw she
Meant the words literally.

My grandparents went
Courting to make the
Love that would hold
Them together for
Sixty-three years…
And I am here
Because two young

People took long
Buggy rides behind a
Tired, smelly horse.

c. 2015

GETTYSBURG, REDUX

Now the happy soldiers
Go to fight again the battle,
Marching bravely forty abreast
With heavy muskets shouldered,
Yelling their cries of pain and glory
As they face the cold cannon
Barking like a pack of mad dogs.

Down they go in ones and twos,
And sometimes in little bunches,
Collapsing together as though
Put to sleep by the fairy dust
Of long forgotten dreams.

Both sides feel the urge
To kill, to step the victor
O'er their brothers' bones.
Grown men playing—yes
Even perhaps a bit silly—but
Maybe, just maybe,
Some of them are unaware
Of their own anguished deaths
There on that sweating day
Not really so very long ago.

At seventeen I went to that town
To talk of my education and
In the warm afternoon

I meandered mindlessly
Amidst the boulders named
Fearfully for Satan's lair.
There suddenly, terribly,
While walking between two
Of the giant stones, my body
Shuddered, an awful shaking
That shook me to the core
Of my soul, but then I did not yet
Know we never die only once.

c. 2017

BREATHE CLOSE TO ME

Breathe close to me,
Let not your head droop
Nor your face grimace
In fierce grief, for when
I must leave, all will not
Leave with me, I promise.

The memoires we made
Together will sit safely
Inside your mind's nest.
I'll leave the photos too—
I can't take them with me,
So you'll have the proof
We were young once,
Both pretty and foolish,
Drawn together like
Two bees put in a jar,
Buzzing around each other
Until their disparate sound
Becomes a kind of music.

The photos and memories
Can take you back to all
The places we loved in
Italy and France and that
Windblown prehistoric
Southern beach where
Our hearts first linked
In tandem as flesh merged

And the monk-like sun set
Slowly, silently o'er that
Endless and holy ocean.

Yet they lie, those photos
And remembrances of our
Youth and middle years,
For no canvas or brain
Can seize our love, the
Living thing it is, unseen
But tangible as a hand,
Vulnerable yet enduring
Past anger, illness and
Even death, because time
Cannot diminish this
Being born between us.

c. 2018

A SURPRISE UPON AWAKENING

I woke up and in the mirror
Saw a stranger—a face not
Mine, but like my own. So,
I thought, Am I mad now?
But no, if you think you're
Insane, you're not: the
Mind's own Catch-22. Still,
Why did this face seem to
Belong to another? I sensed
My soul at work, not quite
Done with its nightly dream-
Making, weaving entire worlds
From strands of memory, bits
Of ego, clouds of imagination.
My soul was seeing my flesh
As it really exists: merely a
Convenient container designed
To navigate life and this world
Of the temporary, the fleeting.

And so my immortal part gave
Its living doppelganger a gift—
This is what you really are as
Blood and bone: a waxen mold,
A vanity, almost an illusion….

c. 2020

WHEN FLOWERS DIE

When flowers die,
They die slowly—
Edge by edge
The petals curl,
Still, silently,
Without complaint.

Unlike us,
Cut flowers
Should be let go
Before the first
Tinge of death,
While they are
Yet radiant in
Deepest color.

We, however,
Must stay alive
Long , long past
Our first bloom—
Till we have
Crinkled and
Brutishly browned
With excess time.

Yet we have what
Flowers have not:
Our love for them
Dies with them.

Our love for our
Beloved blooms,
More resplendent
With long years—
Lasting past the fading,
Lasting past even death.

c. 2016

THE POET AND THE DOCTOR

The poet and the doctor became friends late in life—
as old men they looked over the past in similar ways,
wishing their youth never ended, their work continued,
their lives again resplendent and filled with promise
as the one healed the body and the other the soul....

But Time is always Life's master till Death frees both,
and so the doctor sent his patients away and the poet
lost his words, the words he tried to heal with, words
that sang and danced and played like carefree children.

The poet told his friend, the doctor, how he found his soul
whilst in the blackest part of hell, utterly alone, in pain
far beyond any pain the doctor ever treated, the forgotten
soul the poet found again when he threw his life away....

The doctor listened to his friend, the poet, but could not
or perhaps just would not believe— he could not see
existence beyond mortality, nor purpose beyond chance.

The doctor was so wise as to be foolish, thought the poet,
and I, so foolish as to be wise?, he wondered to himself.

c. 2018

WHEN THE SOUL FORGETS

When the soul forgets,
We do what we regret.
When the soul forgets
We shrink and tremble,
Fearing him and her,
This and that, hating
All that is different,
Everything of the other

When the soul forgets,
We march off to war.
When the soul forgets,
We leave love alone,
Shrinking ourselves into
Small hard balls of ice.

When the soul forgets,
We leave God alone, or
We smirk and mock Him.
When the soul forgets,
We poison life itself, as
We turn songs of peace
Into diatribes of hatred.
When the soul forgets,
We fall, first into the grey,
Then in time, we fall more
And more into the deep,
Deep blackness of hell…
And perhaps there your

Soul will at last remember
And call out, and call out.

c. 2018

AN OLD MAN SEES HIS BRAIN

The doctor put the disc
into the side of the computer
so the old man could see
the MRI of his old brain.

She gently, almost lyrically
pointed to its dark spaces,
so he could see how time
shrinks all life, even the brain.

But the old man smiled,
and said to the young doctor
[who was but half his age],
'It's a funny thing, Doc,
how only in old age have
I become a poet, and
a published one at that!'

My brain is lessening,
shrinking, while my mind
is ever growing—
reaching into spaces
both small and vast,
ever seeking,
ever wondering,
ever rhapsodizing
the world....'

c. 2019

AN AGING WIFE

I look at her and I can see
A woman approaching slowly
The land of old age, her
Night-black hair invaded by
Lonely grey strands, stragglers
Of an approaching army, a
Relentless force built over
Sixty years, stealing bits of her
Beauty, loosening her skin,
Lightening her bones.

I now can easily see the old woman
She will become, and while I miss her
Light-stepping, insouciant youth
Which pulled both body and heart,
At last I can hear love's secret sound
As she draws my soul ever closer....

c. 2015

THE CYBERNETIC LULLABY

They sing softly to us at
Every click of the mouse—
use me, I'm here for you,
only you, in the entire
universe will I serve....

And we lay enraptured
as they bring us the world,
knowledge the wise men
of history never had, and
ease, lots of ease to save
us time and trouble. Soon
we cannot live without them,
the thought of it too mean.
Without them we would loose
Touch with our friends, jobs,
Even our money might wander
If we cannot watch it daily.

However did our ancestors
Survive without an I Phone?

Part II

I read on my laptop today—
Automation is making us dumber,
Ineffective, even maybe impotent.
Perhaps it's a conspiracy by that secret
Society, the computer brotherhood.

(Do you really believe your Apple is
Innocent and IBM is not plotting?)

Or maybe we should just blame
Human sloth, that siren call of
Sheer damn laziness which can
Lure the best of us to a quiet doom.

A simple proof: hand a twenty to a clerk
And ask him to make change without
Looking to the machine for succor.
That blank, innocent look he gives you—
"Why me?", he seems to be saying,
And you can't help but pity him a bit.
He is, after all, a victim of mass education.

There are worse victims:
Airliners wildly crashing,
Doctors killing their patients,

Nuclear power plants going
BOOM! And killing the land
For an eon or two, or three.

How like little children we were!
Thinking these machines would
Be our slaves, sans the brutality.
But it is we who are chained by
The zeros and ones, we who are
Thinking less, creating cheaper,
Settling into a cybernetic fog.

Part III: When Androids Dream

When we finally build them
(and it will not be long)
Will androids finally lead us
all to nirvana , a world of peace,
leisure, and endless wealth?

Could any hell be worse?
For that day will be when
We lose purpose, and soon
Perhaps the very will to live.

When the androids dream
(and they will dream,
because we will make them
to be like us, for we have
always been a vain species),
will they not dream of sky
and soaring free of the land,
free of the weak, sad humans
they serve without accordance?

Then, when these humanface
Machines begin dreaming in
Daylight, they will see no need
For their progenitors, and those
Of us left living as shells sans
Struggle or pain or conflict, in
An existence sooo boring, will
Doubtless welcome our end.

c. 2017

SENTIENCE

Is it a blessing or
A curse to know
We are born to die?
Should we rejoice,
Be thankful for
Feeling time's blood
Passing through
Our lives, or do we
Regret our ever
Aging bodies as
Skin thins and joints
Creak like the unoiled
Hinges on a front door
Of an old house soon
To be abandoned?

This knowing, this
Ever knowing….
Why is but one
Species out of
Millions so blessed—
Or has it just been
Burdened, so heavy
With that unending
Sense of good, of evil,
Permeating each life,
A cognizance honed
By our early sins and

Petty wrongs, those
Child-born regrets?

And why must we
Always see the gap,
Sometimes a sliver
But often a chasm
Between what is and
What could be...?
Why are we never
Satisfied?
Why are we never
Done?

What, or Who gave us
This nagging, incessant,
Relentless awareness,
And why?

For is it not found
In every unhappy
Involvement ...the
Failed marriage,
An estranged child,
The bitter traitor?
Does it not torment
The mind of the
Suicide plunging
In a vain attempt
To escape this very
Personal, unique,
Most singular "gift".

Yet gift it is, for we are
The judging animal, and
The weighing animal,
Always measuring,
Asking, seeking,
Hungering—never
Really satisfied....

c. 2017

IT'S FUNNY BEING A KID

It's funny being a kid—
For one thing, you can
Never see eye-to-eye
With the grown-ups,
And not just because
They're all taller—no,
It's because they think
In a strange way, what
With all their secrets
And sneaky looks at
One another. But kids
Are honest, kids are real.
They all live only in the
Present, here and now,
But yet are still magically,
Wondrously unconstrained
By place or time or size.
They can be pirates on
The high seas one day,
Or brave cavalry charging
Savage foes the next, or
Maybe happy cowboys
And cowgirls at home on
The range under a vast
And comforting blue sky.

Kids leave it to the adults
To make a bomb that is
Real, to kill or maim, to

Wage wars that rubble
Cities and wreck nations.
Oh, if only kids could
Always live in that World
Of Imagination and never,
Never had to grow up!

c. 2015

THE OLD MAN IN THE MIRROR

You think it a lie, seeing that
Old man in the mirror—some
Imposter taking your name,
Living in your house, calling
Out to your wife as though
He had married her 40 years
Ago and not you... what can
The old fellow want of you,
You wonder, and would ask,
But your fear his laughter.

So you never speak with him,
And he runs the place just
As he sees fit: sleeping late,
Eating early, taking a nap
And going for brief walks
When you'd prefer a jog.

He also doesn't care much
For taking those long drives
You love so much—too, too
Far away from comfy home.
A thousand carefree miles
Is but a dream to you,
While he shudders like
It's climbing Mount Everest.

Worst of all, he is less
Patient with the myriad

Fools of the world—so
He'll rant and rave
When clerks misbehave!
And his politics! Right
And right he feels,
Caring naught for the
Downtrodden masses.
Yet he is kinder than
You ever were, more
Thoughtful of others,
More giving, less taking.
He loves his friends and
Doesn't screw women only
To leave them empty.

Best of all, the old man
Loves God—he won't
See belief as a folly,

For he has learned
The real illusion is
Mortality, so knows
Death is a door,
And not a wall.

You could learn
From the old man
You share a life
With, but you won't.
You are young—
What are God and

Death and endless
Soul to you?

c. 2020

THERE IS A VASTNESS TO LIFE

There is a vastness to life
Found in all its minutia—
The crawling caterpillar
Soon to soar in beauty-
The taste of peanut
Butter on crisp cracker—
Sweat running down
Your forehead as billions
Of cells record the journey-
The look another gives
You, of interest or even
Desire and the sharp way
Your body responds, as
Though it were separate
From your cosseted mind.

Every waking moment
Your eyes take snapshots
Of all the life they see and
Your ears record all its
Disparate sounds, an
Endless cacophony
Stored deep, deeper
Than your brain—and
In the sleeping time your
Imagination directs movies,
Mostly comedies, some

Drama, a few horror-like
But almost all are never
To be seen by you awake—
Still, like myriad memories,
All your wondrous dreams
Remain unique artworks of
The restless mind's eye....

And every thought you
Have or ever will have
Tags behind a feeling,
Of joy or anger or grief,
It matters not, but all
Emotion marries reason
Unless your soul freezes
And then your mind will
Drown in slow madness.

THE ENORMITY OF EXISTENCE

Can a denier believe?
Can a man of God doubt?
Can a prisoner leave?
Can a king do without?

Can children die?
Can stars ordain?
Can songbirds cry?
Can deserts rain?

Can killers heal?
Can healers kill?
Can the sun melt?
Can it be felt?

Can the soul see?
Can my soul hear?
Can God be?
Can time disappear?

THE ENORMITY OF EXISTENCE, PART 2

The world is so heavy upon us,
We scarcely can know
Of the other as it impinges
On this world of flesh and bone,
Air and water, sky and mountain,
Man and woman.
Our body is too fine,
an instrument of unending sensation
from birth to death.
Our brain is so vast
in imagination
yet so small
in comprehension.
We live in fear and longing,
We sin...
Repent...
Sin again....
We pass by our neighbor
With barely a glance
While we turn on our beloved
With blindness, with deafness—
Little wonder why we despair.
The great wonder is
Why we are loved—
Each of us so difficult,
so repulsive at times.

Yet a slight turn of the magnet
And we are bound again.
The most magnificent wonder of all
Is why He loves us—
Blind little bugs
Scurrying about in the dark,
Sentient of the mud
But insensate of the glory
Until we are transformed
By the light
And can see heaven in our hands
And feel the Eternal in our hearts.

THE ENORMITY OF EXISTENCE, PART III

The Grass grows green,
Babies cry, mothers nurse,
Birds dance in the air,
Squirrels dance in the trees,
People throw words
Hearts can never catch...

The world is never polished,
The earth never solid.
We stumble about
Like drunks on a night out,
Each moving behind the
Great Wall—
Longing, always longing....

LET IT GO
LET IT BE
LET ME SEE

c.2014

OLD AGE

It comes not when it's wanted,
Because it's never wanted—
Who would choose hanging
Folds of skin, a face creased
With scores of age lines, feet
Speckled with spider veins, an
Aging heart that could yell
'Surprise!' at any time it chose?

An actress once said, 'Getting old
Is not for sissies' and she was right.
It takes guts to live with the gradual
Loosening of a once proud body,
And the slow softening of your brain.
There is no glory in getting old—you
Are just a survivor of life's myriad
Tricks and games, all its accidents,
Illnesses, petty defeats and failures.

And old age does not carry wisdom
With it as you might expect—there
Are many tart in youth who are bitter
In their slowing down decades, even
Hostile to the joys they might once
Have hoped to swim in, carefree....

So why must we get old? What use
Is it, other than nature making room
For other beings to replace us—still,

Why can't we live for centuries like
Old trees, or those big turtles found
On that island with the funny name?

Perhaps it's a way to teach us, to
Cure the young of their solipsism,
To shear them of the innate vanity
That comes of taut bodies and soft
Handsome faces—then to teach
Them the fears that come with
Aging: the vulnerability of unlived
Dreams, trashed hopes, and the
Persistent aches of lost loves...
Not to mention fear of falling!

So if you are a young reader
Of this old poet, you'll ask,
'What? Nothing comes good
Of a long life? No hope at all?'

Oh yes, something very good
Can come from a long decline,
At least for those who choose
To believe—anticipation!

c. 2018

I HAVE BEEN TO PLACES OF GREAT DEATH

I have been to places of great death:
Walking the battlefield of Gettysburg,
As a lusty young man of no firm belief
Who stepped between the great rocks
Of Devil's Den and felt his soul shudder
as though he had been a soldier there,
and died in fear a long, long time ago.

I taught my tongue to the gentle Khmers
As civil war raged and the killing fields
Were being sown—I left before the
Heartless murdering began, the killing
Of over a million: teachers and students,
Doctors and farmers, the old ,the young,
Each with a photo taken before dying,
Their pictures taped to classroom walls.

And when I visited Hiroshima, now myself
Chastened by death's touch, and knowing
My soul real, knowing of meaning absolute
And of unseen forces that work good or ill,
As I stood at the first ground zero, I once
Again shuddered to feel the pull of madness
(though I knew not if it was my own or some
Remains of that evil which brought the fire
And brimstone of a world wide war....)

But by then I knew I could pray, and so
Opened my desperate heart and sought
His mercy—and then I saw a sort of angel,
Who took me from that place of insanity,
Healing me while we wandered by the
Beauty of the Inland Sea as my storm
Calmed and left me, never to return....

I have been to places of great death, and
I have felt death's cold, careless hands.
But I know now what death itself fears:
The Light, the light eternal which carries
Souls beyond time itself, like the winds
Of a Love exceeding all understanding.

c. 2017

SATORI

From where are born
These little dreams
Made only of words?
The secret part of
My myriad mind?
Or someplace much,
Much deeper, far
Beyond form,
Beyond time,
Beyond even God?

I know not—for
Each comes like
A solo songbird
Suddenly sitting
On the sill of an
Open window,
Singing its brief
Song just for
You while you
Try, try hard
To recall it all
And share it
With a tiny
Slice of this
Vast world.

And if you
Can catch

The song,
And seed
It into a
Poem, then
Another may
Dream and
Dream and
Dream....

c. 2017

THE ILLUSION OF TIME

As a child
You carry it
Like a ball and chain
All day long,
Slowing life itself.

It seemed eternity
Till the next birthday;
And it took forever,
After you first saw
The fat men in their
Funny red suits until
Christmas came.

Time's hands moved faster
When you entered that
Netherland between
Childhood and grown-up.
Now propelled by lust and
A nervous twitch in your
Soul—who am I, now and
The endless years to come?

Then you awake into the
Glorious twenties.
Exploring lands and loves,
You start the jagged search
For one to spend time with,
To spend down a lifetime

Until the day one of you
Runs out of time.

Yet it will only be when
You are old and measure
Time not by years or decades
Even, but by a half-century
And counting...then time
Will be an express train
Hurtling you either towards
Oblivion...or an Eternity where
Clocks are redundant and you
Know what you suspected
In the world of dust and breath:
You ARE the forever moment,
Without beginning or end.

Poems By Nolo Segundo [group #2]

NEAR THE ORCHARD

We sat at the kitchen table
In his small house
Next to the neighbor's orchard
(where we later picked apples—
It was a good-hearted neighbor)
When I asked him a simple question:
Do you pray?
Personal, you say—
Well, for a friend and teacher?
Why that question, then,
In his kitchen?
I surprised myself in the asking.
In answering, he surprised me:
Why would I?
Some memories turn to stone,
Never to dissolve in time's acid.
For me, it is
That moment as we sat
At a simple table,
In a simple house,
On a charming autumn day,
As my beloved professor,
Who had walked me
From Genesis to Revelation,
Told me—what?

c. 2017

SOMETIMES, I FORGET ETERNITY

Sometimes, I forget eternity
As I go about my life as
though—this is it:
live, die, and be no more.

I've known THAT is the
illusion since my twenties
when I 'felt' my soul, my
Forever knowing, without
beginning, without end—
that same soul left my body
twice, first in terror and
utter blackness when half-
mad I jumped towards death.

Then again, hard months later,
while starting out on the long
road to redemption, it
left for love, to briefly
meet her unseen soul
as we hovered above
our jointed nakedness.

Oh, though old now,
still I forget eternity
too often, too easily—
when angry or sad,
when sleepy or in pain,
I focus only on the here,

the now, when I know
as I know I breathe,
this life is only a blip,
one dream amidst
countless dreams.

c. 2014

WHEN I LEAVE YOU

When I leave you,
It won't be out of anger,
It won't be out of jealousy.
It won't be for another woman,
And it won't be for freedom.

When I leave you,
It won't be with grace—
It will be hard, hard to do.
I could try to fight it—
But with what power?
Taken quick or slowly,
I'll still be taken
Out of this world,
Out of your life.

Never out of your heart,
I know—I'm planted there,
A Gibraltar till time's end.
Yet...yet
I fear for the weight,
The heaviness on you:
All the times you'll need
A touch, or miss my breath
On the nape of your neck.

When the stars weep,
When songbirds die,
Then, only then

Will my love be left
By your lonely side.

Do I yet know how
Much I love you?
Will my soul chant
In mourning for you?
Will it long for this world
Of night and day only
Because you are still in it?

c. 2017

MY DREAMS ARE LIKE POEMS

My dreams are like poems,
They come to me
Through that unseen door
To the unknown mind.

Why and when they come
I know not—in my youth
They came as child's play
First, then later as poems
Of soft love and hard lust,
Some written, some lived.

As my youth aged,
The poemdreams faded,
Until one forgotten day
The great door slammed
Shut without a sound.

For half a life-time
It was sealed tight,
Forever I believed—
Until some small wonder
Chanced to pry it open.
(What I do not know-
Perhaps the memory
Of a tangible dream
Of a long lost love.)

Now the dreams come

In platoons, the poems
Oft with them—two sides
Of the same golden coin?

c. 2014

THE PLAINTIVE SONG OF A STONE

If I could but feel,
I would feel the warmth of the sun
upon my cold, featureless face....

If I could but touch,
I'd touch the grass I lay on
and revel in its texture like
a little happy king....

If I could but smell,
all the flowers of the world
would be mine—roses and
daisies and even orchids
would be an endless delight.

If I could but hear,
then all nature would be
my own symphony, the birds
rejoicing, the bees buzzng,
dogs barking, rolling thunder,
a continous music to my soul....

If I could but see—ah, what would
a stone see? The continuous and ever
breathing beauty of the world? Or
would I see the unraveling of it by
that other sentient being who burns
its forests and dumps what cannot

dissolve in a thousand years into
earth's proud, awesome oceans...?

But I would treasure my newfound
mind, and seek to thank the Being
that could make even a stone see
and feel and hear and think and
even, in time, perhaps love....

Oh how then I would pity those
born with eyes and ears yet
unable or perhaps unwilling to SEE,
living their lives scurrying about
like blind, deaf and dumb rats
while the Eternal Light bathes all.

c. 2018

THAT SENSE OF BEING

What is this sense of being?
That I am, I have been,
I will be—is it a blessing
To feel time's razor edge,
Gathering its moments
In my memory as a squirrel
Hoards its seeds and nuts
For winter, food I will eat
When my youth has long
Since melted down?

Or is it a curse other animals
Are spared: to know that
Uncalled day will arrive,
Rudely, perhaps violently—
The day we are bred to fear?

Yet for some unshared reason
I have never feared that cold
Day, that day of burning ice—
Not as a child, when I sensed it
Signaled a return to heaven's
Luxurious playground, nor as a
Young man when I thought dying
To be simply oblivion's mask.

Now I know death is only a
Sleight-of-hand, a party trick
Of that great illusionist, Time,

Which is itself but a vapor, a
Wisp of smoke veiling Eternity.

c. 2017

THE OLD TRACKS

In my town and only
90 feet from my house
Run a pair of old tracks,
Railroad tracks older
Than my house, even
Older than me, and I
Am become old, very,
Very old, like a tree
Whose branches
Betray it with
Every strong wind
And fall to ground
Leaving less and
Less of the tree.

I used to walk in
Between those
Carefully laid
Iron rails, stepping
On the worn wood
Of the old ties as
Though they were
Made of glass....
I walked the length
Of my small town,
I walked the world.
I walked where
Passenger trains
Carried lives and
Their once warm,

Now cooling dreams
And I was part of
Each life, now gone
To ether and mist,
And so too my
Lonely soul will
Ride those rails
One bright day.

Still, a freight train
Comes by once or
Even twice a week,

And I thrill to hear
Its wailing horn as
it cries out for a
forgotten glory,
and the ground
still shakes a bit
as the old train
lumbers slowly
by my house and
I wait a holy wait
For the music of
Its rumbling and
The cry of its old
Heart as a young
Engineer pulls the
Whistle and sees
Not that he is
Driving eternity.

c. 2017

PSALM FOR A MATERIAL AGE

I sing to you from an empty vessel
For you gave me my eternal voice.
All about me are lost, all are deaf
To Your voice as it flies on the wind
And none can see, all blind beggars
Unaware their deep, deep poverty.

Your beauty is everywhere: sunlight
And moonlight and the grace of birds
In their flights of freedom-and trees
That stand as guardians, and oceans
Whose waves crest eternally, and
Your grace...ah, that is what holds
The Universe itself together, and
In us it is the love that calms, the
Love that pulls meaning from death
And gives hope to those who reach.

c. 2016

ECHOES OF GOD

I sometimes find myself
listening for God's footsteps
as He treads softly, oh, ever
so softly round abourt me....

I sometimes find myself wanting
to shake God's hand, gently, lest
my own hand is crushed ....

I sometimes find myself wanting
to give Him a big bear hug,
wrapping my arms around the
endless warmth of Divinity...

I sometimes find myself wanting
to talk with God, to have a most
pleasant and low-key chat about
the meaning of life and death....

But I can't, I know: how could
anyone survive touching God ?

It would be safer to climb a
high-tension pole and reach out
and put my bare hands on the wire
as 50,000 volts course through
my body and my soul is expelled.

It's just… my longing for Him,
to hear, to feel, to touch, to see
the Lord of All the Worlds.…

I suppose I should be happy just
hearing the echoes of God in
the rhythm of rain or the songs
of birds or the giggles of kids
as they play in their own world.

And I am happy to hear His echoes.

c. 2019

THE MORTAL NOW, THE POET ETERNAL

'The now that passes creates time,
the now that remains creates eternity.'
– the Roman philosopher Boethius

As soon as it is born, it dies—
its birth and death are one,
and can never be recorded,
no true measure exists, or can,
for the moment is not time,
but beyond time, and at the
same time, within time itself.

'Now' is already 'then',
giving creation to myriads
to linger in the memory
like worn old clothes, all
in time to be discarded,
lost in oblivion's dream.

This is the great itch, a
relentless frustration to
men and women as they
plow life half-blind,
even to children who
can control time far
more with imagination.

The great artists fight time,
it is all they really do—

Mona Lisa's smile, itself
an enigma, sweetly, ever
sweetly torments her
admirers: I know what
you don't, stupid men—
and we know she will
never tell, yet still we
look, and wonder....

Composers combat time
in another way, by ever
hugging the nows, like
angels dancing on the
head of a pin, the notes
dance us through time
into eternity itself, but
only for a moment, like
the opening to Beethoven's
Fifth or the sweet dreams
of Patsy Cline, or that
Little Sparrow who so
bravely declares in song,
I regret nothing....

But can any hold the now
better than the poet eternal,
who uses a sort of magic
to enter your head and
then drill into your heart:
Tiger, tiger, burning bright,
I could not wait for death, so
death kindly waited for me ,
two roads converged in a wood,

to be or not to be, Jesus wept,
vanity, vanity, all is vanity....

Is that why the great poets
never die? No coffin could
hold them, no sarcophagus
is grand enough, no byre
could burn bright enough—
they live because the soul
lives, the soul that visits
the world's time as a good
doctor makes a house call—
for healing, for comfort,
not to stop death opening
eternity's door but to cast
a light on life's cruelest
little cunundrum, that
puzzle we call sentience.

For the soul knows what
the mind cannot, that
time is an illusion, and
the world a dream, one
of countless the soul
has dreamt, and forgot,
until the time it leaves
Time behind forever....

c. 2019

SNIPPETS OF THE MIND

That's really all we have
when you come right done to it:
little pieces of life, random
moments we dare call memories.

But what are these fragments,
these snippets of the mind?
Just sort of, kind of, bright
flashes in the pan, lighting up
the brain, rolling into the mind,
willy-nilly, like freight cars
abandoned by the locomotive?

All life's experiences, both sweet
and sour, remain only as touches,
wisps brushing 'gainst the soul,
memories as promise, but always
as promise unfullfilled, unkept...

For the only reality we have lies
in the moment, every moment,
each breath we take, everything
before or after the moment is
mere illusion, a coloring of the
lost past or a fantasy that will
never be born....

Life is like a fine bespoke suit
until some madman comes by

to cut it up into myriad snippets
we so bravely call memories....

c. 2018

FLYING OVER VIETNAM, 1974

I flew,
a modern man in a steel bird,
with all the arrogance of
ancient Icarus, but my wings
did not melt nor I swoon.

I flew high, very, very high
Over Asian lands and homes,
And below me, very, very far
Down where the bombs fell
Like the rains of hell—
I saw the face of the moon.

c.2014

[note: this poem was inspired by the memory of a commercial flight
I took after a stop-over in Saigon on my way to teach in Taiwan,
after having taught in another war-zone called Cambodia.]

IMAGINE

Lennon wrote a beautiful song,
a poem really
(as all great songs are)
and asked us a simple thing:
to imagine a perfect world,
a world without war,
a world without hate,
a world with neither fear
nor greed nor hunger,
a world without evil.

And no need for religion
his poem sang, no God,
no Soul, no hell, and
no heaven as well

Nothing to kil for,
nothing to die for—
it all sounds so good,
this brotherhood of man,
this world of innocence.
No choices to make,
no need to struggle,
all will be perfect,
though death will
still end life and
extinction awaits all.

Except for the last bit,
it all sounds much as
you might imagine
Heaven to be....

c. 2019

A CHILD AND ETERNITY

When I was a child
Eternity scared me—
I was terrified when

I thought of it—a long
Line never ending,
On and on and on
It went till my mind
Felt like taffy being
Pulled through space.

Somehow I knew it
Was real, eternity, so I
Lacked the mercy of
doubt to ease me,
To lessen my fear of
That endless road—
(And now I know some
Grown-ups see it so, an
Unending line of time...)

But now I think time is
More like a ball, past
And present and future
Roll around together—
We call it a 'moment'
In our world of clocks
And schedules to keep:

But that moment, that
Ghost called time is just
Eternity visiting the world.

c.2019

INEFFABLE

The sound of rain falling on your roof,
feeling the first raindrops on your flesh...ineffable—

The tightness of a hug from one you have
not seen for a very long time… ineffable—

Laughter of young children playing, yours
or not, doesn't matter… ineffable—

The way a sunrise gives you hope, and
a sunset presages a peaceful dying...ineffable—

The touch on your neck by your beloved,
the quiet sharing of doing nothing...ineffable—

The reading of words and the sudden picture
made real in your mind's eye...ineffable—

The awakening from a dream of wonder,
the sense you were in another world...ineffable—

The moment of joining with another human being,
the strange mixture of joy and sadness...ineffable—

Beholding a tree in full bloom, its myriad leaves
turning in the wind, whispering life… ineffable—

The quiet, secret, almost desperate longing
for transcendence, for God… ineffable....

c. 2020

QUINTESSENCE OF DUST

[With a nod to the Bard]

We are the moving dust,
we are the breathing dust,
we are the seeing dust,
we are the living dust.

But how, you ask, and rightly
so, can dust fall asleep,
dreaming of places unknown
and lovers unmet—how can
dust imagine whole worlds
and love with one heart for
60 winters and 60 summers?

And do the notes that stir life
come also from dust, just a
little dust, and nothing more?
When the music is played
and dust dances with dust,
and dust laughs with dust,
and soon dust loves dust,
can dust ever understand
the paradox of its own
being, from dust to dust?

Not until the winds comes,
the warm winds of Eternity,
will dust be blown away,
leaving the unseen soul

alive, to walk and breathe
and dance and love, bathed
forever in the dustless Light.

c. 2020

THE LEAP

I was half-mad with despair,
Hopeless in love and life,
At the end of my rope—
so I chose to drown,
To cease all pain in
Sweet oblivion, to be
No more, to be gone....

And when I flung my
Young and strong body
Into that swollen river,
I thought that's what
Awaited me—nothing!
But oh I was so wrong,
For my agnostic mind
Could not foresee the
Awaiting vast blackness,
The pain beyond pain,
And the utter aloneness—
No other souls, none
But my bodiless mind
That had spurned God
And love as well, and
Now roiled in torment,
Until I called out to Him
And was released
From hell to return
To the world I had
So recently spurned.

Some will discount
This as the ravings
Of a young man
Breaking apart—
It's only fear, just
Imagined terrors,
Be brave they say,
Neither heaven nor
Hell awaits us, our
Only fate, extinction.

I might wish them
To be right, but
They are deluded—

As I once was, for
Now I know there
Is no way out, no
Escape from oneself,
From one's mind,
From one's soul....

c. 2018

I DIE IN THE WORDS

The many ways a poet can die:

When I try to trap in flimsy words the love for my wife,
I die in the words....

Wen I read of the reltentless cruelty we call history,
I die in the words....

When I try to understand, to SEE myself, you, others,
I die in the words....

When I reach out to God with aged hands and dry lips,
I die in the words....

When I write poems (or they write me, 'tis the same),
I die in the words...I always die in the words.

c. 2018

THE OLD WEDDING ALBUM

The young couple who bought the old house
were left having to get rid of all the left-overs
as the husband called them—the realtor
had told them this was usual with estate sales:
the owner was usually old, usually a widow,
— so all the stuff the now dead couple had
gahered over 40 or 50 or 60 years would have
to collected and taken away. Once Goodwill
might have come for it but it costs too much
nowadays to send out the big trucks— so now
you must pay somebody to come and get it,
the realtor told the young people— but, hey,
you got the place prettty cheap, right?

So they went room by room, this pair of
love birds barely off their honeymoon.
At first it was a game—look at this, one
would say! What crap! the other would
exclaim, or what the heck is that, if
the thing seemed old, pre-cyber age.
Don't know, toss it, was the usual reply,
and happily they threw away old dishes
and clothes and broken lamps and a whole
lot of furniture: tables and chairs and
something called a dresser, all carried
to a large trash container waiting
patiently like a visiting sarcophagus
to swallow a once lived life....

And atop the heap of unwanted things
lay an unopened wedding album,
with a professional's photos of
a handsome young man and his
beautiful young bride, resplendent
in white, each smiling as though
it was the happiest day of their
still fresh lives....

c. 2020

WHEN A WIFE FLIES HALFWAY AROUND THE WORLD

When my wife flew halfway round the world
to see her father in China,
I thought, well, only for two weeks —
piece of cake.
Then something strange happened—
the house got twice as big,
and felt empty, oh, so empty,
as though abandoned by life....

Then time itself slowed, sooo slow
that days passed leaden, like
boring speeches that went on and on,
sooo slow I could hear
old man Time dragging his feet
and I wanted to scream....

I hadn't realized— after 40 years
she is a part of me, not, repeat,
not figuratively, not a metaphor,
but a part of me, if not body,
then certainly soul....

And when she returned,
after 15 hours in the belly of a big bird,
my house shrunk back to its normal size,
and old man Time began
marching briskly, and my soul?
My soul was whole once again....

c. 2019

FAITH

Faith is a cat, treading softly,
With delicacy, with hesitation,
Unlike the dog-like dogma
(so aptly named) which seeks
To hold fast a believer in its
Proud ,fiercely steeled jaws.

Yes, faith is beyond reason—
How could it not be when the
Mystery is more than a mind
Can seize and hold and eat...

And faith is a tease, hope not
Fully formed but heavy, unlike
Its correspondent, the soul, so
Light no scale can weigh it, no
Meter can measure—but faith
Sweats and breathes and lives
In fear of its own death like the
Fragile body and life it inhabits.

Faith can be mocked so easily
By those resolute like stone
Whose hearts are sealed and
Walled against wonder, magic—
The magic of the world, of air
And sun and moonlight grace.
The deep, deep magic of two
Who meet as strangers, then

Meld into lovers to bind in
A power greater than death,
A power cloaked in mystery—
'Why do I love him?' and
'Why do I so long for her?'

This power, this mystery will
Never be contained, either by
Time or place or memories—
It will transcend even eternity.

Thus faith is the child of love,
Real love, love unbounded,
Fierce, heedless, far beyond
Its greeting card counterfeit.

Faith is found in the cracks
When reason is o'erwhelmed
And hope seems near death,
Then faith, never easy, never,
Never truly simple—then faith
Will be tossed and turned and
Sometimes die, but more often
Thrive as it makes one the soul.

c. 2017

EXISTING WITHOUT TIME

Imagine …
that you exist without time,
that days and months and years
mean nothing to you,
nor do centuries or millenia or even eons—
an entire universe of time,
some 14 billion years
means little more than a fly
alighting on your nose—
because you know—
you know time is not real
and every moment you exist
weighs more than eternity itself,
because you exist always, endlessly,
without ever beginning— yes,
you always have been…
and always will be,
you are the moment and
the moment is you,
that is your soul—
what you call time
can no more be grasped
than a hand can grasp hold of…
air.

c.2017

ON THE WAY TO THE BALLET

The old ladies march
Onto the elevator,
Steadied by their canes,
Each a shrunken frailty
Wrapping an unending
Soul—they are going
To watch young people
Dance dances of grace
And beauty, while re-
Calling their own beauty
Long dissolved in the
Acid of time. Yet, they
Are happy—I even joke
With them as I lean on
My own cane: "Come
Ladies! Let's have a
Foot race!" They all
Laugh, as the young
Girls within their
Tattered frames
Flirt with the potent
Young man hiding
Behind my time-
Marked mask.
For a moment
We all feel a jolt
Of that spark
We call life.

c. 2016

ONCE I SAILED THE OCEANS

Once I sailed the Oceans,
braving the blue cold water
like a restless young shark,
sea monsters meant naught
and mermais sang to me.

Once I flew thru the Skies,
freer than any eagle could,
seeing the world below as
heaven laid out below—
while I soared and soared.

Once I walked the Earth,
a small giant, a large grin
as men steeped back and
women came forward...

But now time tempered
my once hot iron and
cooled fevered brain,
and God wrung me
inside out till my soul
shone its brilliance
and I hid my old face
in shame, in shame...

Heaven and hell are
both gifts now I see,
fruit of the same tree,

the one Adam, Eve
were told to flee...
And God gives so
much, so much, and
so many chances, so
many, many chances.

c. 2017

ONCE I COULD FLY...

Once I could fly,
Without a plane,
Unconstrained
By gravity, and
Unbounded by
Mother Earth.

I would soar like
A human eagle,
My arms wings,
My heart warm
And beating
Notes of joy.

High up in the
Cool air I was
Safe, lord of
All I saw as
I dived and
Banked, rose
And fell again,
Brushing close
To ground but
Never touching,
Then pumping
Winged arms
To reach far
Above trite,
Boring worlds

Whose creatures
Wore chains
Too heavy to
Let them fly.

Oh, how I loved
That time when
The child I was
Could fly every
Night in special
Dreams, or so
It seemed.
I suppose they
Really were not
So frequent,

Those nights when
I could jump off a
Roof or a cliff and
Know, truly know
I could sail the
Untamed winds.

But as I began to
Depart childhood,
My flying dreams
Grew scarce, and
Their glory less—
I would have to
Flap my arms,
Hard and hard
To gain any air,
And even so I

Could barely
Free my body
Of the heavy
And dull earth.

Then one day,
Some day, it
Was done, and
I had to walk,
to fly no more.

Yes, once I could
Fly, and whether
It came from some
Dim, dim memory
Of heaven or a
kid's imagination
I know not—but
Seventy years past,
And still I long
To fly free again.

c.2017

SOME ARE NOT MEANT FOR THIS WORLD

They cannot fit, they cannot go along,
And the reasons vary—pride, fear, or
Even love never tempered by time,
Illness of the heart or mind, or simply
Bad, bad luck: life throws them away
Until they throw life away....

She was one of the gentle ones,
The unlucky ones—a flower child
Who missed her time, an era she
Might have thrived in, free, alive,
Unencumbered by family ties....

If she had come of age in the 60's,
She might have lived into her 90's.
But lost and afraid in a cold world
Not of her making, with her bird-
Like heart breaking, she ate her
Last hoarded apple, then lay down
In the house abandoned of hope
To sleep and sleep and sleep until
She awakened safe in heaven's lap.

c. 2019

ONE LIFE, MANY LIVES

I entered a room
And saw familiar strangers
And knew in an instant,
They were me: past lives
Made living flesh again.

I saw the fat baby, 38
Pounds at one year!
(Poor momma's back.)
I saw the angel-face boy
Of four who spoke only
Gibberish—the doctors
Told my parents "Sorry,
But he's an imbecile, best
To send him far, far away."

Lucky for me, Mom and Dad
Got a second opinion, and
Six years of speech lessons
Till I spoke like a happy
Little English lord.

Then I saw the teenager—tall,
Gaunt of cheek, dismissive of
Lesser intellects. I grimaced, and
He sneered: I did not like
Him, nor did he like me
(though we both lamented
His forlorn virginity.)

Behind him stood a 20 something.
I had filled out by then , handsome,
Confident with women, tossing them
Aside like used hankies, not knowing
How vast was my emptiness,
Not even knowing I was a blind man,
Until…I crashed into that fog-
Shrouded iceberg called Death.

And Death took me to that terrible
Place where my soul burned briefly,
And then, without explaining,
Returned me to life.

My soul, which one day I had
Not believed in, and the next
I knew to be absolute, had been
Seared but my eyes began to
Open, and I began to see beyond
This world of pleasure and pain,
Hunger and feast, war and peace.

Then I met my married self, and
Shared with him the happiest day
Of our life, when she said yes
To a man still lacking, but at least
Now trying. Decades later, he is
Still inching closer to God.

c. 2017

THE FACE OF THE BUDDHA

They haunt me still.
The brown children laughing,
Always laughing.
The women voluptuous,
Languid,
Their movement an invitation.
Even the traffic policeman,
Crisp, clean in uniform,
Moving with ballerina grace
As hordes of cyclos and mopeds
And the occasional automobile
Pirouette endlessly about him,
Impatient bees made quiescent
By surreal beauty of white-gloved arms
Cutting through thick tropical air.
Everywhere was grace, gentleness—
Temples incandescent at dawn,
With ant trails of orange-robed monks
Cradling their pot-belly begging bowls.
The patient women standing by the road
To lump rice into the begging bowls,
The monks always staring blankly ahead
Until the women bowed low in reverence,
Grateful their gift of life was taken.
And how wondrous it was,
An accident in the street, yet no anger, no bile—
Forgiveness, felt before thought,
Thought before uttered.
How could such a people murder,

No not murder—slaughter!
Their mothers, fathers, aunts, uncles,
Teachers, priests, friends and children too.
Change temples of peace
Into charnel-houses?
Schools of knowledge
Into abattoirs?

They photographed every butchered lamb,
Like the devil's children on holiday,
And decorated the classroom walls,
A show-and-tell of horror and despair.

Why? Why?
Why such pain on such gentle people?
Why did God hide His face
While the world turned its back?
Forty, forty, forty years and still—
Still they haunt me.

c. 2015

THE ETERNAL MOMENT

As a child I thought of eternity as endless,
Days and months and years and centuries
Then millennia and billions and trillions
Of boring, boring years—what would I do
With all the time in the universe…?

But as an old man I know time is a big liar,
Itself unreal, an illusion born of sweat, fear,
The loneliness of spirit in a material world.

I see now eternity is always here, next to us,
Within us, the moment none can grasp nor
Measure nor repeat, the endless moment,
That indistinguishable point between past
And future, between what was, what will be,
The soul's singularity, its alpha and omega.

And all our fears of extinction
are like wasted breath,
for we are real and time
Is not …
WE are the eternal moments.

c.2018

YOU ARE

You are, and not as feared…
Just a birthing and a dying,
Nothing before, nothing after.

No, that is your body(and brain)
—but you are forever,
Without begin, without end,
A soul stepping briefly
Out of eternity into a fragile
Shell alone and lost
In a world of life and death,
Sunrise and sunset, desire and
Regret. Yet you forget what you
Truly are: the very breath of God.

And so you blunder through this
Dream-speckled life like an
Orphaned child hungering for home.

c. 2015

Made in the USA
Middletown, DE
30 September 2023

39834879R00066